1973

kent

A CHOICE OF ATTITUDES

A Choice of Attitudes

By GRAY BURR

Wesleyan University Press

MIDDLETOWN, CONNECTICUT

Acknowledgement is gratefully made to the following periodicals, in the pages of which some of these poems were first published: *Chimera, The Diliman Review, The Massachusetts Review, The New Yorker, Poetry, The Quarterly Review of Literature,* and *The Tuftonian.*

The poems "After the First Refusal," "The Aggressor," "The Butterfly," "Challenge and Response," "The Fallacy Revisited," "A Family Chronicle," "Fulfillment," "Genesis," "The Lover Questions His Love," and "The One and Only" were first published in *The Massachusetts Review.*

The poems "Sailing, Sailing" and "A Vision," the latter in slightly altered form, were first published in *The New Yorker.*

The poems "Meadow Remembered" and "A Glance at the Album" were first published in *Poetry.*

Acknowledgement is also gratefully made to the following companies, which published books in which certain poems first appeared: Basic Books, Incorporated, publishers of *Of Poetry and Power* (1964); Doubleday & Company, Incorporated, publishers of *A Controversy of Poets* (1965); and The New American Library, Incorporated, publishers of *New World Writing #1.*

Library of Congress Catalog Card Number: 69–17790

Manufactured in the United States of America

FIRST EDITION

FOR ELLEN

Contents

A CHOICE OF ATTITUDES

What We Listened For in Music

We heard the phoebe calling in the wood
Two notes as pure and clear as abstract love.
Platonic call, I thought, speak to us of
The far, the true, the beautiful, the good.

Again two notes, these more pellucid still,
As though some angelus of heaven rang
Against our earthen sense, and, ghostly, sang
Of all that our corruption could not will.

We stood a moment there, rapt, yet appalled
Until an answer came: two notes as rich,
As absolute, but on a deeper pitch.
Then we knew that earth to earth had called.

After the First Refusal

After the first refusal, consciousness came.
The flowers flared; the sun blared like a brass.
Beast and bird slept their beatitudes.
To man alone fell a choice of attitudes.
Man fell alone to a knowledge of his name.

And the earth revolted, marched against him then,
Against the only thing that knew, that could
Conceive an opposite, make Will a fool,
In even that vise of a hand be a turning tool:
Whatever the cost, the curse, Man would be men.

Lost was the likeness of lions, the dullness of doves.
Original Sin stared down with a murderous smile.
"Give them an inch of knowing, they'll take a mile,"
Something said, that no longer wanted their loves.

A Skater's Waltz

There was a pond on which we learned to skate,
Where the blades flashed like sabres, and the ice,
Scored and carved as an old dinner-plate,
Lay locked within its shores as in a vise.

How different we all were; how much the same.
Do you remember Speed, the hockey ace,
Who shuttled stick and puck to early fame?
Not one of us could skate to match his pace.

And there was Flora, queen of pirouette,
Who wore such scimitars upon her feet
And whirled her skirt to flowers; oh, well met,
Flora, lovely Flora, light and fleet.

Hand in hand, the couples zigged and zagged
And had their ups and downs; the cut-ups fell
Most often, though bad holes were plainly flagged.
Still, anyone could trip and break the spell

That music made, and movement, in the mesh
Of skaters shifting, threading warp and woof.
Oh tapestry of heart and mind and flesh,
We all were skeins in you; yet one, aloof,

Hung from the general scene, our loosest end,
A mystery and reproach to naïveté.
You'd meet him coming round the sharpest bend,
Racing against the crowd, another way.

Whistles shrilled in that well-ordered place
And he was often asked to leave the ice.
But when he'd gone, so also had some grace,
Some figure only he could improvise.

I think that if the god should pull that thread,
A whole woven dream might fall apart.
It would, at least, be less. Arise, ye dead!
Remain, O Dionysian, in our heart.

A Birthday in the Desert

The milestone mildly passed;
Another year used up.
The rattler added a rattle,
The tree another ring.
The chorus watched the cast
Fight a losing battle.
Life withheld its cup
And death rehearsed its sting.

I drove through the day's heat.
The sun crept round behind
And giant cacti raised
Their asymmetric arms
Like soldiers in defeat.
Whose years were defined
Here where the land, crazed,
Died on abandoned farms?

I saw the sidewinder
Eyeing me from her dune,
The Gila monster shake
His brilliant abstract back.
Fool's gold glowed like tinder
Where earth began its moon;
To the Great Salt Lake
Led the map's cul-de-sac.

My buzzard thoughts had dined.
Shadows began to reach
Gigantic fingers from
The mountain peaks behind.
Night lay dead ahead
Across this sealess beach.
From dark to dark I sped,
Going where I had come.

Meadow Remembered

The bridal daisies and the goldenrod
Wreathe in that meadow where rare afternoons
Came flowering from our richest summer sod.
Our wills were watered there with rilling tunes

Of birdsong, and with tilling touches we
Prepared the grounds of all we later thought.
Then our joined land made greater seigniory
Than the world's manor we had separate sought.

And starflowers so confused themselves with grass
It was as though the constellations whirled
About our dreaming heads, the old impasse
Dissolved and heaven mingled with the world.

Levitated meadow, bowing stars,
Have sunk and risen since you went away.
The earth and sky are back behind their bars;
Our flesh of grass is burning into hay.

The Epistemological Rag

The world turns and its turning wheels
In sprocket with the chain of years.
The Dipper falls and disappears
Behind the mountain as it reels.

The plane of the ecliptic rides
Through all the signs of Zodiac.
Orion hunts and Cygnus hides.
Hunter and hunted won't be back.

In fusions of their furnaces
The supernovae forge new planets,
Byproducing universes,
Heavy elements and granites.

Hominids are somewhere breathing
Methane, argon, other gases;
Ecologically teething
Atoms gather to new masses.

What does it all mean to humans,
Men and women, you and me?
Are we really catechumens?
Our first text this galaxy?

Must we try to piece it all out
With new math and heavy taxes
While our dunces juggle fall-out
And the earth slows on its axis?

Saints and devils short-cut mystery,
For the rest it's grope and die.
Though we can't predict our history,
We have got to make it. Why?

Otherwise there is no moral
Save that time becomes the hero,
Man a fancy, earth a coral,
Dualism double zero.

Questions of the Afternoon

All the caked and frosted lawns occlude.
Across the street a neighbor geysers snow
From a machine. This time's an interlude
Between my classes and where else I go.
The sun is falling to a level with
The world. No longer high, nor low,
It stabs into my vision with a myth.

How shall I take it? Glasses rob its round
Of glare, but then its brilliance is reduced.
By staring straight into its eye I've found
I had to close my own, while pale and fused,
Its image slowly faded from my mind.
By such devices are we disabused.
How can we choose in which way to be blind?

The neighbor clears his walk and strikes a light.
A puff of smoke, and he's inside his house.
And now his curtains close against the night.
Is his the image that I must espouse?
Do not these south sea islands, beach hotels,
And sunlamps under which we brown and drowse
Provide us with insipid heavens, hells?

Is there still mystery in the dying sun?
And do its wheels of myth, in slowing down,
Do so to turn us toward some brighter run?
If so, then its corona is a crown.
Who was it that the Greeks at Delphi heard
As they were starting in to build the town?
Apollo? And did they believe his word?

20

A Family Chronicle

Here on huge blue mother's skirts I tread,
Flecked by her petticoats of spume and foam,
A step-child of her almost endless dead.
Inside her swim my cousins, still at home.

Our fathering sun's intense and tropic stare
Includes more paramours than I can know.
Some branches of the family grow rare;
Others may live on Venus, Mars, Pluto.

This sand is skeletal with what remains
Of unsuccessful lines that lost the prize.
My fingers sift the vague ancestral grains
Of those who wrongly chose to specialize.

The brainy porpoise, the enormous whale
Still live, unlike some relatives on land.
Who would have thought that size was going to fail?
Or that, unaided, mind can't understand?

Of all my siblings, only the clever squid
Kept really supple members free to use.
But, having done so, that was all he did.
Those who stay with mother play to lose.

Great-uncles and great-aunts along the boughs
Have fallen of their weight, or stayed the same,
Or vanished in the trunkline up to us
Which strains toward change, development, and aim

Beyond survival to what destiny
We cannot calculate except in dreams.
The primate's thumb that salvaged energy,
The ape who rose, have left to us what schemes?

The evolutionary hero stands,
The family heir, richly unspecialized.
One cerebrum and a pair of hands
Are hereby willed to him, bequeathed, devised

That all men by these presents now may choose
How they shall ply the family heritage.
Whether to take their chance, or to refuse.
How young we are; how dangerous the age.

Garden Puzzle

The window-screen sifts the blue cumulus
From my cigarette.
I sit and ponder the big synthesis but the answer
I just forget.

Constellated at my feet newspapers pepper
And salt the truth
I taste in them nevertheless as I squirm and shift
From the rage to the ruth

Of the somewhat helpless who is and who is not
Quite able
To say "Just kill the witches and you'll be a lot
More comfortable."

And against much advice I read in the Bible
A love-lorn column
With wish then to use such passion and scruple without
Getting solemn

And queasy, but can't do it, and the mixed-up
Jig-saw
Puzzle cut from the Garden and scattered in a world
For the cat's-paw

Mankind to put together in the pain of its truth
Stays shining
More dear, derelict, strict though asunder
Than all our repining

Has learned. I must hope that solution mankindled
May find breath
Wiser than any we know, if the solving's a matter
For life, not death.

Preface to a Family Album

To look again at old photographs is to see
Time personal cut to bits, a sight reduced
To visual footnotes of private history.
Appropriate, then, is the blackness of album pages
Which, broad obit borders, rightly set off
A disconnected notice of death by stages.

Here how we looked in glossy prints returns,
Each a detail blown up out of all proportion
To the full montage, and yet in such small urns
Of sight the past lies buried and embalmed.
On this page, look, the grandmother so excited;
And on the next so utterly becalmed.

The pages turn; the child we were grows up
In leaps so monstrous as to seem a trick.
Just yesterday, one thinks, they took that close-up:
Long-lost freckles, squint, and vanished cowlick.
Here's the same face later, lost in shadow,
Under a battle-helmet, the eyes hectic.

So many shots, self-conscious, stiffly posed,
Tell no more of our life than its clichés,
Which is to say our deepest truth's exposed
Here in these picnics, wars, and wedding days.
An album never lies, leaves that to those
Who don't like pictures taken of their ways.

25

Genesis

The primal work was nearly done.
A hand ripped out an excess range,
Dropped a sea there in exchange,
Reached an aeon, lit the sun,

Then with a gesture made a park
Too perfect. In its absolute
A mind mislaid an alien root.
Slowly the sixth day grew dark.

In the evening, just at rest,
A face like Asias without span
Twitched once with the tic of man
But smoothed again, the thing expressed,

And turned away to other skies,
Already musing on a sun
Where something better might be done
And, conceivably, more wise.

The Aggressor

He was that battlefield of muddy, torn,
And bursting earth we all have sometime known.
A civil war begun when he was born
Ravaged the land between his blood and bone.

Upon such country crops would never grow.
His sun was fever and his rain was sweat.
Troops of his being froze in bloody snow
Or drowned in seas of tropical regret.

He found no middleground. No armistice
Was ever signed between his impulse and
The enemy dilemma's terms of ice.
His heart took on the look of No Man's Land.

Thus savage was the scene. How would it end?
When would the slaughter of the self be done?
Only the foreign wars would ever mend
A civil conflict that could not be won.

Landscape

Whitecaps fleck the lake with abstract gulls.
A gang of Adirondacks hulks across
The middle distance where they stop the eye
From farther travel. Every loss
Implicit in this scene is personal.
The colors of all memory go dry
And yet this landscape bleeds whenever I
Pass it in the gallery of my sight.
Like one of those *Pietàs* adepts shawl
Against the profanation of the light,
Darkly it hangs upon my private wall.
And in a prayer I say the real gulls fly
Over the water where their mirrored selves
Drown in that reflection of the sky,
Those actual fathoms where the pickerel delves
And slashes at the trinkets flashing by.

The Fallacy Revisited

"Summer is over," you said, and here and there,
As though they had just understood your words,
A branch began to burn, sumac to flare,
And an oak released a southbound flight of birds.

It was only that we noticed weather then,
In the sudden chill, not that we thought the season
Implicated thus in the plights of men.
Pathetic so to think we are told by reason.

But, if discrete, we stood in an apt setting,
Suited, nonetheless, by leaf and blade
That seemed to share with our hearts a great bloodletting,
And we walked, appropriate, in the dying glade.

The Damned

Raw ulcers and his aspirin signify
Love lost and loose as a cannon splintering
A hull, as, decks awash, and foundering,
He staggers up the sheer of a wave as high
As childhood's surge to shores he never reached.
And he hungers for a speech that might unsay
The flesh marooned, the ghost forever beached
On a small uncharted island of dismay.

Round him shoal waters heave and crash.
Birdflights cut hieroglyphs in a sky
He may not read. At night reefs gnash
And rip the bottoms out of dreams, and the Dry
Tortuga of his day drains all his leaf
As the sail, forgiveness, shrinks to a handkerchief.

The Butterfly

Tracer of wind's contour by line of flight,
His weightless leaves of color caper in air.
How rootlessly his color grew wings' flair:
You've seen him shut

And open and shut in slow winks on a twig
Or a cannon where he can most thoroughly please
By irony our taut taste for antitheses.
For he's not big

And, soundless, opposes the burly and loud. When
Children fish him from blue air he shapes
By crisp of wing, their love, like ours, is perhaps
Too crude to plan

Fit action for its object. He can't last
Without a sting. But now his jerking yellows
Puppet the eye in the wind's blue shallows
And purely contrast

The dull arrest of things. He is a locus
Of precision's myth in whose dissolving change
The worm climbs wind and we the range
Of all our focus.

The Wealth of Hills

This lavish hill has spent itself on flowers.
See how the squandering ground has flung its purse
And poured into the wind how many myrrhs
Where jewelweed and the goldenrod have powers

More to enrich the gaze than the gathering.
Our sight is debtor thus to spendthrift sod.
Beloved wastrel, Midas of petal and pod,
Your golden touch becomes your bankrupting,

I thought, but every nodding flower meant no:
They were on loan to seed a fallow eye
But they'd be drawn to dungeons by and by
As ransom for the prisoner of snow.

How praise enough the largesse of this hill?
Show us again that the giver is most wise;
Fill us with flowers up to the top of our eyes
Before a miser winter shuts the till.

Two Dualists

Crusoe, when enisled,
Dreamt a new England where
Blake's Jerusalem
Would blaze in smokeless air.
Nevertheless, he took
Gun and knife in hand,
Cut and shot his way
Back to old England.

Raleigh in the tower
Thought clearly about
Love, Life, Death,
And how best to get out.
A poem set him free
Once he got it said.
Only an ax could part
That body from its head.

Huckleberry Finn

To round a wound with fiction, the scared brat
Came of age at fourteen, ripe with luck.
Or honor, seeding in the river-rat,
Bloomed with the river till near Cairo Huck
Stepped from the deep seam that had sewn
A heart to patchwork states. White unto black
Knit in the double voyage that he took.

One by one, the rotting towns were strung
On the boy's sight. On the river's vine,
Hanging four thousand miles of continent,
The colonel's sneer leaked blood and the swung
Earth ate black meat and fertilized per cent.
The King and Duke, endearing picaresques,
Were only clowns of greed behind their masks.

The Devil had got him, he knew, as the quality
Had warned. Tension of childhood mixed
Property with blood but the lithe heart flexed
Its river-rich sinew and bent his muddy
Fathom to a friend. History fixed
In a leash of money, its cunning animals,
The indelible gene pinning its murderous fables

To the fabric blackened on a spitted earth,
All dissolved in a boy's blue summer
Once. Now whitethatch could with mirth
Twitch horror's eaten face, go broke,
Mock mummied pedants in the red shimmer
Of learning's whoring gown, trim what he spoke
To fit a shrew's bluepenciled mouth.

34

Robin Hood

Robin Hood,
When I was twelve,
In your greenwood
How I would selve
Myself, rob rich
Legend to give
Poor everyday.
With you I'd rive
The willow-switch
And our sword-play
Left Gisbourne in
A bestial skin.
And with you, hale
At the Blue Boar Inn,
I drank brown ale,
Clanked nipperkin
With Allan-a-Dale,
Took Stutely from
His gallows-cart,
Saw Sheriff pale
And King smart
When finger and thumb,
Unmatched, would loose
Clothyard shaft
And the grey goose
Feather flew
And arrow sang
A song more true
Than art or craft
Or history knew.

Eyestrain

We thought how carelessly he'd asked
That every day be sharp and drenched with light,
Nor wanted a moment of vision masked
But begged for depth and clarity of sight.

And did so still, but now was glad
To see in the sun the bite of an eclipse.
And all of us noticed a habit he had
Of peering, on glaring days, through tinted chips

Of glass he'd taken to carrying, and how,
When high noon shrank the shadows very small,
He'd blink and wince and a squint would plow
His face with furrows, till, last of all,

Whether a day was cloudy or well-lit
He stayed indoors and didn't look at it.

The One and Only

He heard the flicker drumming in the wood.
It sounded different. He began to march
In a route step nobody understood.
Oh, Emerson, perhaps, with half an eye
Cocked upward and the other fixed in starch,
Caught glimpses of him as he shambled by.

He did a lot of travelling in Concord,
Mapping his progress as he went along,
Finding a pond an ocean unexplored,
Two rivers that were never truly charted,
A stretch of beach the surveys had all wrong:
Where standard maps left off, his atlas started.

Leaving to sheep their skins, to towns their ways,
He built a school because he felt perplexed;
Enrolled, and stayed there just as many days
As needed for a general education.
First he learned, and then he wrote the text.
Next term the course was open to the nation.

Many have applied but few have finished.
And none has ever quite achieved his rank.
Originals, in our day, have diminished,
Are frowned on rather, knocked about, and cut.
For luck like this, Thoreau would have them thank
Whatever gods have jarred them from the rut.

The Difference

The one nasturtium that survived the frost
And that I tended faithfully every day
Was, I began to see, already lost.
In the same way

A dream that was as carefully set out
In what I'd hoped would be a rich corner
Of heart and mind became all withered doubt
And its suborner

The same, plant for plant, and place for place.
Too little sun and water, stony soil,
Unseasonable nights and darkened days
Conspired to foil

Each which as a seedling promised much.
When now I go to pull them up by roots,
The one comes easily, its feeble clutch
So little suits

Its need to stay in earth, but as I grasp
The other's massive growth in straining hands,
Even in death I feel its spreading clasp
Through all my lands.

Moth Craziness

Last night some moths flew up upon the screen.
It was a light within that drew them there.
Whether they were to see it, or be seen,
Was all the question yearning made unfair.

Embroidered by the night upon the mesh,
The wings upon their bodies were too weak
To force the barrier and allow such flesh
To occupy the brilliance spirits seek.

Some grew quiescent; others, frantic, beat
Their dusty paper wings against the wire.
Though all the night was theirs as a retreat,
They chose to be imprisoned by desire

And would not wait till day, when every flight
They made might have the blessing of the sun,
But had to know the artificial light
In which their silhouettes fell one by one.

Fafnir

This ornament can square himself away
In whorls of sinew neat as flemished line
And pile in bracelets an India-rubber spine
That with a spasm can undo the day

It took nine months to lace into a man.
This limbless lizard or this wingless bird
That was in the Garden such a fatal Third
Is now in the great declension Saurian

A small irregular noun that we construe,
According to whim, to be more happy than
The croc, less real than dragons, an also-ran
In the race of fauna toward success and you.

He rises, dubious as a question-mark,
From the Hindu basket on a Bombay square
And does a hipless hula in the air
To show how frivolous menace is when the dark

Child we are breathes music through a reed.
Old Fafnir waits upon our harmony
To grow small as a garter and set us free.
To know our coil is mortal. That is what we need.

Tree of Heaven

Ailanthus from the greenest islands came
To root in soot, in city backyard trash,
On any pinched, forsaken urban foot.
Breather of smog, ill-fertilized by ash,
What ironist bestowed on you your name?

How do you live where weeds will not take root
In soil one shade more arable than stone?
On dishpan drinks and smoky doles of sun?
Unyielding exile, why do you atone,
Sharing with Adam an ill-favored fruit?

On Beacon Hill where little courtyards bask
In your Moluccan shade whose shadows trace
And sift the cobbles for comparison,
You are blown broadcast like a scattered race
For whom survival is a special task.

Exemplar of all orphans, you can sow
A fine-grained wood and evil-smelling flowers
And shape to shields the scars where branches were.
Brother to city men, your life is ours
And far from heaven is the place we grow.

Nature and Art

Shallows slosh over rocks with a washing sound;
The wind in pine and birch is riverine;
Lakewaters, skies, and shores enclose a scene
Cezanne might paint, though his were more profound.

Simpler and more complex his canvases
Than any camp New Hampshire has to show.
One sees this rough arrangement whirl and go
Perfect in some picture where its masses

Balance as they never can in nature,
Where light is better made than even sun
Can manufacture here, where every ton
Of terrain mends the landscape's nomenclature.

A prince of paint, a lord of light and shade,
Has made a point: nature defers to art.
So the mind feels, and eye, but still the heart
Will keep the living summer, though ill-made.

Greetings

Day after New Year's Day. How to assess?
Who can thunder no, or smile a yes

At all the variations of a year?
Or mark the cloudy days off from the clear?

"We were alive through 1962"
Would be enough for Montaigne, me, and you.

Two attitudes, conventionally, are struck:
The optimist's for sticking, the unstuck

Warns of perils yet to come, and fakes
Resolutions that he gladly breaks.

It was a year, like any year, of crisis.
The world skated where the thinnest ice is

And all could hear it crackling underfoot.
But just before the crust of earth was put

To tests unprecedented, skating back,
Humanity avoided the last crack

Of doom and now is on familiar ice,
The cold war rather cozy, almost nice.

As for our separate histories round the globe,
They ran the same in New York as in Kobe

Or any place, except for superficial
Differences, official, unofficial.

We've had our ups and downs. The loved and lucky
Helped us out, as did the lost and plucky.

How individuals beg for generalization!
We love to stereotype a man or nation

And thus be rid of complex multilevel
Men and lands the which our minds bedevil.

We pigeon-hole by précis or cartoon
And even make a man out of the moon

Rather than face that waste without a face,
And may have oversimplified the place.

By rounding on my method, I cut short
Many large assertions. I abort

Further all-inclusive general statement
Which had been going on to say what hate meant,

And love, in your specific situations,
By synthesizing this and other nations'

Men and women, lives and loves and such—
But suddenly it seemed a bit too much.

How did your last year go? I couldn't say.
But Happy New Year to you, anyway.

44

An Apparition

Looking like some terrible still-born
Unwanted foetus of the mindless sea,
A giant jelly-fish, uprooted, torn,
Wallowed in the shallows helplessly.

Out of its element, stingless and dead,
Ready for gull and cormorant it lay.
Tchelitchew might well have done this head,
So full of dying dream, so rich a prey.

Mauled by the sands and wrestled by the waves,
It was as if intelligence itself
Had been defeated in the deep-sea caves
And banished from the continental shelf.

And here it was, a plaything of the tide,
Rolling its gelatins in cloudy masses
As though it dreamt on after it had died,
Unable to extinguish some Parnassus

It had conceived of when it floated free,
Or so had thought, above the ocean beds.
Looking back, I could see two or three
Insatiate seabirds tearing it to shreds.

Sailing, Sailing

It is the sea's edge lubbers love,
Where sand, the mirror, slurs their faces,
And the surf's smash completes the cove,
At least from an observer's basis.

Such people like the harbor's hull
That rides so steady in the swell
And never lists or pitches. Lull,
Not squall, for them, means sailing well.

But we have known some sailors who,
In a seaway mauled around,
Didn't dream of Malibu
Or catboats on Long Island Sound.

A lot of commodores in whites
Foundered on the yacht club shoals
While Captain Slocum's riding lights
Danced a jig between the poles.

Eye

Only the eye can drink
From a lake a mile away
Or climb ten mountains in
Less time than it takes to say,

Land on the moon, the stars;
Fall, rise, hurdle, sprint;
Put a lid on the world
Or narrow it to a squint.

Lover of light, whose lies
Deceive us, doctors say,
Let physics chew surmise.
Dine out on the crusty day

And drink the sun's gold wine,
Devouring all that seems.
From color, form, and depth
Concoct your optic dreams

And give them to the mind
As its best evidence.
Then only, thought may grind
A harder sharper lens.

Bluejay and Mockingbird

Today the jays still wrangle round the house;
Crested birds who savage others' young,
Dressed in eighteenth century soldier's blouse,
Fierce and medieval, brash of tongue.

Slashed with chevrons on their quick blue sleeves,
Absolutely certain of their flight,
They challenge all the wood, revoking leaves,
Calling wren and sparrow out to fight.

With martial clangor and incessant rage
They fill the day with whoops and rebel yells.
Hoodlum in all but looks, on the rampage,
They murder first our patience and then hell's.

Though many birds fall silent at their jeers,
Some do not. The mockingbird is one.
His is the song the bluest jay most fears.
It makes him bluer still, and half undone,

To hear in mimicry with something added
The image of his war-cry made absurd,
Twisted, lampooned, lilted, aped, and padded
Till he himself becomes another bird.

Self-pity, or, My Cat Is Dead

Your tongue was rougher than a file
With which you rubbed your kittens smooth and dry.
How silly that I could cry
For you when I
Smelled a hundred thousand dead
Rot in the wind.
If all the salt in the sea
Can never wipe the wind quite clean again
Of you, for me,
Then war's unkind enough, though I, unkinned
By it, had not a tear to spare
From struggle to survive.
But when I think that you are bare
Of breath who were so quick alive,
(Death only was more spry)
Like me, a lover of yourself and laps and sleep,
And since you tell me I will one day die,
I know a cause to weep.

The First Leaf

The first leaf of a coming Fall
Untimely fell the blaze of July.
I couldn't think of a reason at all
Why it foolishly blenched and loosened to die.

A friend took a forty-five
And shot himself. He'd said he would.
Who'd seemed to me boldly alive
But much I had misunderstood.

I think that I could tell him now
How pinched he felt in a crowded wood,
How hunters had notched the parent bough
And forest fire had seared his mood.

I ponder Robinson, leaf who fell
From bright midsummer long ago
And wish I could go back and tell
How sorry I am that I didn't know.

Harbor Impression

The gull's wings were white sabres drawn on the blue day
And if the harbor looked like a mouthful of wreck,
Wind-scratched waters were slow tides of gooseflesh on face,
Ships had left heartbreak here, drawn by exotic beck.

But there was dry delicate smell of sun on planks,
Likewise sunsmell on asphalt, exhausts, hoods of cars;
Odor of sun on seawater; shadows broke ranks,
Skittered in swirls, chips, wind was chisel on waters.

Shadow and sun stippled water with dark and wink.
Sun burnished spots of shine but black chips of shadow
Lurked under lip of each tiny wave, mesh with chink
Glints, the sun sown buttercup thick through the meadow.

But gulls slid down air like rich children laughing swerve
Down marble, though under reckless flesh gaped nothing.
Easy, accustomed, no need of luck nor of nerve,
Though below duskfall whipped seas with toxic frothing.

While night's nearness drew drudge from tug, ashore lights flamed
Fire from wire strung deep in the city's core. And here
An old gull sheathed wings and dozed on a pole, sleep-tamed:
Ballooning from darkness, close now, he dreamed of fear.

Rumination on $\phi(x^1, x^2, x^3, x^4) = C$

One has to take math on faith,
To say nothing of metaphysics.
The past is the present's wraith
And the future's time-bomb ticks.

How hard, then, it is to say,
If these are simultaneous,
What is meant by our stay
Or going, and how extraneous

Or central our drama is.
$E = mc^2$
But what can we make of this
Footnote beyond its clue?

What seems to be more certain
With each advance in science
Is that truth, however plain,
In theory or appliance,

However jiggered and tinkered
With by our top mechanics,
Isn't ready to be inferred
But only implied by manics,

As we sometimes call our best.
Superb achievement by one
Is such a check to the rest
Few can bear the comparison.

But no matter how animal man,
It's hard to think his tensions
Aren't more the result of than
The cause of four dimensions.

Yet what this notion means,
i.e. whether new equations
From somewhere in our genes
Will be our next evasions

Or will somehow recall
Causality in you
And make me logical
I only wish I knew.

Challenge and Response

Wildflowers came up all spring, the snowdrop first,
Then bluet and marsh marigold where not
A hand had planted for an eye athirst.
A beauty so gratuitous begot

A kind of debt. Disorder's gift, unsent,
Was yet received and cared about till thus
The season's fragrant petalled accident
Found end in us, an aim in aimlessness.

Unmelting petals from the apple tree
Like lightest snow lay in the green grass,
Deepening with their winter mimicry
A sense of summer coming on at last.

But merely to wait and watch the making weather
Had never been enough. I'd take a hand.
Put in a rose or two. We'd work together.
It was a challenge I could understand.

A Glance at the Album

I saw only the edge
Of a photograph peeping out
Of the album: as if a ledge
Had given way in the mind,
Back, back, I fell,
Clutching the living-room air,
Down the years' well
To a beach of childhood where
I surprised the lovers behind
Big umbrellas, and buried
Their scowls and bribes in the sand.
(Perhaps they all got married.)
Back to the left land
And bit of unfinished picture
Where little would go as planned.
No art or other stricture
Could order it into a game.
It was a wild unreeling;
Neither an unmixed pleasure
Nor without effect and feeling.
And this photo represents
A time when a kind presence
Let the heart rest a measure
Before what was coming came.

Player to Playwright

Scene after scene, dismantled, disappears.
The characters and plot so intertwine
That the whole play compounds a mystery.
One claque declares the author is divine;

Some critics say the drama writes itself.
A faction still insists the theme is man,
Another that he plays a minor role,
His subplot linked somehow to masterplan.

If incidental, evanescent, he
Declaims as though stage-center were his home.
Under the baby spot of his own sun
His nations speak. Bright Greece and dog-dull Rome

Bow and exit. Enter new personae
Who, in what often seem redundant speeches,
Advance the action so mechanically
As scarcely to persuade or half to teach us

Anything we dream we ought to know.
No one, of course, is sure the play's didactic.
Not all agree it's even a good show
Nor that we know its strategy from tactic.

Author! author! the entangled chorus
Cries, but from the wings no form appears.
Lovers of nothing think that such would bore us.
Our deus ex machina's worked for years,

Though creakily, and lately seems to threaten
To break down altogether and explode.
Ending with a bang, not with a whimper,
Is catastrophic in the latest mode.

Why must we end in either? I don't know,
And trust we won't. O, Philosophic Poet,
Who wrote the universe, or may have written,
And have withheld the meaning, if you know it,

Pray don't spoil the ending, if there is one,
By telling us in less than metaphor
Why it is you've done what you have done,
Where we are and what it is we're here for.

Only in not knowing your intention,
Or in believing that it can't exist,
Are we, as players, prompted to invention,
Whether or not we dangle from your fist.

Who would play mere stately ritual?
Who could compete with knowledge universal?
If we were sure of absolutes, I think
Man the Fool would not be in rehearsal.

A Day at the Races

The heart knocks and tumbles in the ribs.
"Take off the strain," I hear the trainer call.
"Give up your coffee, liquor, cigarettes."
Go back to cocoa, soft drinks, mush and bibs?
I think it possible that life can pall
Once we begin to hedge the body's bets.

Old soma, you have won a lot of races.
By God, the sweats and swinks I've seen you cram
Between the falling odds and bookies' smiles!
I know the jock that puts you through your paces,
The stable whence you came, your sire and dam,
Your handicapper all the muddy miles.

I'll see you wind the silks around a rail
Many a time, adding your syncopation
To the field drumming toward the final wire.
I'll see you stumble, shy, and almost fail,
Recover, find the tempo, and (sensation!)
Cross the finish line a house afire.

That's how I bet, like all who saddle up,
All who love their mounts but ride with whips
And, knowing the other jockeys and their tricks,
Still drink with them from the same stirrup-cup,
Before the fanfare drops it from our lips.

Lumbering

A sawyer can grow wary in his mill
Of figuring the board-feet to be got
Out of a crooked log, which like as not
Is full of nails, and whether for door or sill

To cut the lumber, measuring with his sense
The grain and width and kind of plank to saw.
And so with sentences cut from the raw
Timber of one's own experience.

Such trees of knowledge, though, are knotty wood,
The grain well nigh impossible to gauge,
Difficult to work at any age,
Darkly rooted and misunderstood.

Pithy the boards, with hidden wounds and scars
That mar the finished plank and flaw the work,
Unfit for building custom-house or kirk;
More suitable, perhaps, for darkened bars

Or brothels even, coffins, questing ships;
All structures that are less for decoration
Than for the function of a conversation.
Such things can use those trees down to their chips.

So, woodsmen, to the woods, and lumberjacks,
Sawyers, planers, polishers, and pilers,
If you would be our builders and beguilers,
Select your trees, and spare us too much ax.

To an Unknown Poet

Blessed the audience who
Reads our poems, for theirs
Is the country of poetry, too:

A province of heavy repairs
Going through a maze with a clue
And falling down metrical stairs

To land with a bump against
A word for which no rhyme
Has ever been known or sensed.

And then, as in a canoe,
Bucking rapids of speech,
Being thrown and whirled into

Prose with all one's gear.
Lucky to get out alive
Let alone with any "career",

As people along the shore
Watch one disappear
And think it rather a bore.

How right they are, for them.
No hard feelings, but
If I leave out that ahem

And substitute tut-tut,
Will it mean a trifle more?
Well, try it. And try to cut,

60

As Emily said we should,
In ivory with a knife
Instead of working this wood-

en stiff unwieldy stuff
Of language with a dull
Wit. That's not enough.

Kitten on Two Keys

You, fooling your heart away in parlor tricks,
I see you a chromosome and a continent away;
Your eyes not opals now but Congo moons,
Your claws that flip a catnip mouse in play
Tearing the heads off the white buffoons
That sting and sting and sting you with their sticks.

And you're not just the clown prince of your whims
But a Lord of Bengal and a native god
Who harries the safari's twisting snake
That troubles the Punjab jungle with its odd
Desire to make your rivered blood a lake
And put a final rigor to your limbs.

And as you daintily step to a pan I set,
A water-hole in Egypt falls as quiet
As death: the parakeets grow still,
The frogs subside to nothing from their riot,
The night is striped and sabred hill to hill
Till you come back to kitchens and Kismet.

Weeds Are Flowers

I see the dandelions constellate
A meadow and I watch them blaze to ash
As golden polls go gray in a summer's fate
And bees rummage the blond scalps to cash

The farmer at his local bank. Others,
Like refugees, persistent and disliked,
Pop up on chartered lawns where mothers
Slit their weasands for not being strict

Observers of the rights of lease and zone.
Their blood is milky, bitter to the taste,
And dandelions are very hard to own
Because they root where hearts have gone to waste

Behind façades that fear a single weed
May give away the wilderness inside.
When to conceal becomes the only need
The mildest aberration must go hide.

Let free men give dandelions space!
Think how their blooms make warming wine;
How they bouquet the world of Valentine.
A weed is just a flower out of place.

Life Lived out of Season

This March the twentieth is first of Spring,
The equinox squeezed backward by leap year.
A week ago the pussy willows were
Suddenly standing with their tips of fur
Smaller than baby mice. I saw the clear
Sky alter slightly and a yellow wing

Flare in the line-trees like a striking match.
I think it was a daring oriole
Or, possibly, a tanager blown here
By the big wind and storm, bad judgement, fear-
Forces that give to bird or man a role
Unlooked for, from whole cloth a little patch

Of future out of which to cut his measure.
And yet some birds will have a better reason
For warming winter with a flame of gold,
And just so far analogies may hold
As to suggest that life lived out of season
May, in its contrast, be a greater pleasure

Than one too carefully blended with a milieu.
It's good at times to play while others labor,
To work while others go on their vacation.
It takes diversity to make a nation.
Bright oriole in winter woods, heart's neighbor,
We will not always do what others do.

A Play of Opposites

Philocosmos: Outside my blind a bird lit in a tree.
  The tree, an aspen, mobilized the light
  And half concealed the bird I wished to see.
  I ran to get my glasses from the closet.
  When I returned, that bird had taken flight.
  What kind it was my mind can only posit.
  Already it takes on the quality
  Of something outlined, like the world at night.

Musophilus: It was neither robin, finch, nor crow
  Nor phoenix either, though it almost seems
  To share the latter's will to come and go,
  To be and not to be, to baffle, tease
  The mind's concreteness with the shapes of dreams.
  This bird nests only in uncertainties;
  Your role is played out in the passing show.
  It is my mummeries the bird esteems.

Philocosmos: What rot you talk. I'll catch the creature yet
  In gin or snare or glass, with net or gun.
  Its song was magical, and, as a pet
  That bird would be a conversation piece.
  I'll teach it what to say. It would be fun
  And could, with proper handling, bring in fees.

Musophilus: Your world's already rather in its debt.

Philocosmos: I'd talk the game down if I hadn't won.

Musophilus: I know you think you've had the final word,
              But I believe it's just the last thing said.
              Well, go ahead, and try to catch the bird.
              You've often tried before, if you but knew it.
              The squawks and screeches coming from your head
              Make plain to everyone how well you do it.

Philocosmos: I've taken everything winged, finned, or furred.

Musophilus: But every place you hunt, this bird is fled.

Philocosmos: I'll get it if I have to buy the earth;
              Or conquering the place will do as well.
              I set the price of death, the trap of birth.
              I think you underestimate my powers.

Musophilus: Oh, no. Orpheus sang his best in hell.
              You'll have your moments, perhaps even hours,
              But only time will pay the bird's true worth.
              By then your world will be a cracked egg-shell.

Philocosmos: A dismal prospect for a man of action.
              I have no time to waste on mysteries.
              I round my numbers to the nearest fraction.
              Your nice perceptions bore me half to death.
              You'll never see the forest for the trees.
              For every sigh you heave, I'll sell you breath
              And dearly, too. Be wise, and join my faction.
              A bird that I can't see will starve and freeze.

Musophilus: You were its subject once, and patron, too,
But, as you say, the times have changed a lot.
Our talk, at least, has driven home to you
The fact that your new interests lie elsewhere.
Your character cannot resolve the plot,
Though your one part may leave the
     theme threadbare.
Despite your guns and drums and hullabaloo,
There is no luck out there beyond earshot.

To Martha, in Despite of Logic

Now you are as I was then;
    Much of the road to travel
Through fog, forest, marsh and fen
    And pavements gone to gravel,
Gravel gone to mud, and last,
    A track gone off the map.
Is it thus you'd dream the past?
    Better take your nap.

Did I mention heavy tolls,
    Bridges out, and detours;
Killer curves and wrecker holes
    And your fellow creatures
Hit and spilt along the way,
    The winding mortal trap?
That's the hunting and the prey.
    Meanwhile, there's your nap.

Life's a tragic volume said
    The Greeks and other sages.
Prologue and epilogue unread
    While, in between, the pages
Tell redundant stories of
    Error and mishap
And the many deaths of love.
    Restful be your nap.

What if all they say be true,
   In logic plain to see?
The road, inevitably, you?
   The book, biography?
And every saw and homily
   Dandle you on their lap?
To be is love's anomaly,
   So wake up from your nap.

Double Vision

Contained within its shores, the lake lies low.
On a fair day you'd say a swatch of sky
Had fallen between ten hills, complete with slow
Bowling clouds that wander whitely by

The boat we sit in where our lines descend
A fallen heaven like kite-strings of wish.
Which way is up, we'd ask, who now suspend
From our own hooks below like any fish.

And do we rise or sink into that sky
When caught? Who are the fishers, who the fished?
What did the bait mean that could so imply
A world of would be to the world we wished?

The Lover Questions His Love

You know all the paintings, so I won't say
How the light here looks, and doesn't, like Monet.

And how the flowers, spangling this terrain
Hereabouts are much like those Derain

Once put into a picture that endures
Time out of mind; this place is mine and yours.

We know time as a point, and pointillism
Caught a lot of those within a prism

And made one riverbank into Grande Jatte,
Fixed for good and all by Georges Seurat.

We cannot share our lovely scene, as he did
His, owner whose eye and hand have deeded

Us one of his last best afternoons,
More curved and luminous than toy balloons,

And quite as joyous. Light, in ours, will fade.
Already, edges of it ravel, frayed,

Unstable, and we hasten to depart,
Knowing our life distinct from that of art,

Knowing the figures in this foreground flow
Into a montage, into vertigo.

Yet would we really give one of our days
For all of Seurat's, Derain's, or Monet's?

Fulfillment

If once you dropped in the strange well a pebble,
and waited, hushed, while silence grew louder than sound
till up the dark came at last the tiniest treble
plink of expected sound, then you can know how round
ly you fill my sight at a day's end when,
dwindled by blocks of distance, you first strike
my expectation's wound-up pitch and then
fill all my hollow with a rich low hum
like a plucked bowstring's, but sweeter, more like
a guitar's, struck full of a chord by a strum.

The Question

Supposing, just suppose he could go back
Through life as through a telescope held wrongway,
Back to a tiny clear bright circle of day
Where first, perhaps, his coracle took a tack

Oblique to the rhumb line, in the drift and set
Of tide and current, and wandered off the course,
The watch asleep, wind rising force by force,
And the wheel spinning through a wild roulette

Of all degrees upon the compass rose,
Would he give up the island finally reached
Through a white smother and kniving reefs where beached
At last he lives in animal skins for clothes,

With his parrot, monkey, and goat so hardly tamed,
His home-made spear, his bow, his garden-patch,
Few of whose fruits and vegetables would match
The mainland produce, and all his world self-named?

A Vision

There was a weighty sky that went to pieces
Early in the morning. Broken, it fell;
A debris of cloud falling on landholds, leases,
Clothing bare fields and priming the driest well.

Snow covered the scarring road, the ruin and waste,
The pits of man, erosions of time and rain;
And all that had been blemished, crushed, misplaced
Was white and unified and whole again.

For a blinding moment the absolute was seen
As purity of fact and not of concept.
Immaculate and holy and pristine
In a hymn of snow the world of data slept;

Only to be roused by the slanting sun
That bent upon the scene its heavy stare,
Wearing away the transient benison,
Bringing the City of Man to light and air,

Disrobing the statues in the public park,
Letting the mounds of graves again obtrude,
The whitewashed slum unveil again its stark
Indictment, the church a shabby desuetude.

Next day some snowfall still remained in patches,
In corners out of the sun, in the lee of a wall;
Mottling the landscape as with torn dispatches
Blown from a battlefield beyond recall.

Here and there the snowball fights began
As boys shaped white invective to be hurled.
Night fell and the thaw set in; a last snowman
Melted into the mud and soot of the world.

Dreams

I lean on the concrete,
Looking down at the stream,
And see the sky repeat
Itself like dream on dream.

I see the sky repeat
Its clouds, and blue distance
Falling under my feet,
Until, as in a trance,

Lit by the waterlight,
I can believe I stand
On a bridge of such insight
As has no need for land.

There I, suspended, see
The solar phoenix fall
And rise in the same tree,
The world no more a wall.

And, leaning, I confront
My own face looking down
From the sky's enormous font
Where even stars may drown;

And swimming there, it slurs
In the current of that sky,
Ripples and then recurs,
As though I live and die

And live again to dream
Of the face that leans toward mine,
Seeing beneath its scheme
On the bottom's mud the shine

Of an empty beer can, leaves,
Countless almost, and dead.
Sees them and believes
In the Hudson watershed.

I Think How Once I Thought the World

I think how once I thought the world
    The watery floor of a well
Whose sides, the skies, went sloping up
    Higher than I could tell;
Up to their opening, the sun,
    That framed a sky beyond
Too bright to brook a look of mine
    Although the look was fond.

I thought by death to climb those walls,
    That leaving dross behind,
I'd rise all lightness like a god
    By dropping off my rind.
And hooking fleshless fingers on
    The blue rim's utter height,
I'd wriggle through that blinding hole
    Into the fabulous sight.

But now that I love the ballast no more
    Nor less than the balloon,
Although hard put to give it the weight
    That makes the ground a boon,
And though a moth is at my coat
    And rust is in my eye,
I'll hope the sun's a portal still
    But I can wait to die.

Distinguished contemporary poetry in cloth and paperback editions

ALAN ANSEN: *Disorderly Houses* (1961)

JOHN ASHBERY: *The Tennis Court Oath* (1962)

ROBERT BAGG: *Madonna of the Cello* (1961)

MICHAEL BENEDIKT: *The Body* (1968)

ROBERT BLY: *Silence in the Snowy Fields* (1962)

GRAY BURR: *A Choice of Attitudes* (1969)

TURNER CASSITY: *Watchboy, What of the Night?* (1966)

TRAM COMBS: *saint thomas. poems.* (1965)

DONALD DAVIE: *Events and Wisdoms* (1965); *New and Selected Poems* (1961)

JAMES DICKEY: *Buckdancer's Choice* (1965) [National Book Award in Poetry, 1966]; *Drowning With Others* (1962); *Helmets* (1964)

DAVID FERRY: *On the Way to the Island* (1960)

ROBERT FRANCIS: *The Orb Weaver* (1960)

JOHN HAINES: *Winter News* (1966)

EDWIN HONIG: *Spring Journal: Poems* (1968)

RICHARD HOWARD: *The Damages* (1967); *Quantities* (1962)

BARBARA HOWES: *Light and Dark* (1959)

DAVID IGNATOW: *Figures of the Human* (1964); *Rescue the Dead* (1968); *Say Pardon* (1961)

DONALD JUSTICE: *Night Light* (1967); *The Summer Anniversaries* (1960) [A Lamont Poetry Selection]

CHESTER KALLMAN: *Absent and Present* (1963)

PHILIP LEVINE: *Not This Pig* (1968)

LOU LIPSITZ: *Cold Water* (1967)

JOSEPHINE MILES: *Kinds of Affection* (1967)

VASSAR MILLER: *My Bones Being Wiser* (1963); *Onions and Roses* (1968); *Wage War on Silence* (1960)

W. R. MOSES: *Identities* (1965)

LEONARD NATHAN: *The Day the Perfect Speakers Left* (1969)

DONALD PETERSEN: *The Spectral Boy* (1964)

MARGE PIERCY: *Breaking Camp* (1968)

HYAM PLUTZIK: *Apples from Shinar* (1959)

VERN RUTSALA: *The Window* (1964)

HARVEY SHAPIRO: *Battle Report* (1966)

JON SILKIN: *Poems New and Selected* (1966)

LOUIS SIMPSON: *At the End of the Open Road* (1963) [Pulitzer Prize in Poetry, 1964]; *A Dream of Governors* (1959)

JAMES WRIGHT: *The Branch Will Not Break* (1963); *Saint Judas* (1959); *Shall We Gather at the River* (1968)